Essential Question
How do we investigate questions about nature?

Norman Borlaug
and the
Green Revolution

by Jocelyn Cranefield

Iinke Hamming/Ingram Publishing

Norman Borlaug and his friends were walking to school. On the way, they were caught in a blizzard. Then Norman became **exhausted**. He was cold and tired. So he lay down in the snow.

His cousin Sina made him keep moving. This saved his life. Later Norman said that Sina had inspired him. She made him keep going.

Norman walked to school even in bad weather.

Norman Borlaug was born on a farm in Iowa, in 1914. From a young age, he worked on the family farm. Norman helped take care of the farm animals. He also helped his family grow oats and corn.

GIVING 105%

Norman wrestled in high school. His coach encouraged him to "give 105%." This idea helped him to be tough and strong later in life.

Norman Borlaug is in the National Wrestling Hall of Fame.

Norman went to the University of Minnesota during the **Great Depression**. This was a hard time. Many people became poor.

One day, Norman went a talk by a scientist named Dr. Stakman. Dr. Stakman said that rust **fungus** was destroying crops. If they could **prevent**, or stop, the rust fungus from growing, they could feed many people. Norman wanted to help stop rust. He decided to study with Dr. Stakman.

STOP AND CHECK

Who helped Norman decide to become a scientist?

This stem of a wheat plant has rust. Wind can carry rust from plant to plant.

4

Ted Streshinsky/CORBIS

Chapter 2
Work in Mexico

After college, Norman Borlaug worked for a chemical company. In 1944, his former teacher, Dr. Stakman, encouraged him to help solve Mexico's food shortage.

Mexico had a growing **population**. People needed more food. Borlaug had to figure out how to grow more wheat. This would increase the **yield** of the crop. He would work with farmers and other scientists to solve the problem.

YIELD

The part of wheat used for food is the seed, or grain. Yield is the amount of grain that comes from a piece of land. A high yield means a lot of wheat was grown.

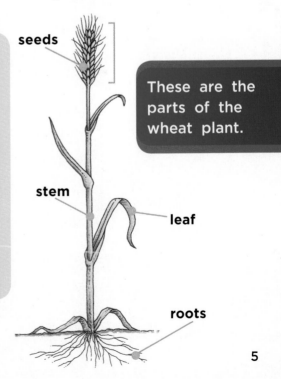

seeds

These are the parts of the wheat plant.

stem

leaf

roots

(t) Tinke Hamming/Ingram Publishing, (b) illustration: Peter Campbell

Mexico had another problem. The wheat was being **ruined** by rust fungus. The wheat could not be used. They needed to breed a new type of wheat that resisted rust. The **process** of starting seeds, growing plants, then combining, or breeding, new plants usually took 10 to 12 years. Borlaug had to find a faster way.

He worked at the Yaqui (*YAH-kee*) Valley **research** station in Sonora, Mexico. Conditions there were perfect for growing wheat. It was sunny. The soil was good. There was enough water for the crops.

Borlaug had a **theory**. He thought he could create a new type of wheat faster.

Yaqui Valley was a good place to grow wheat in the winter. But it was too hot in the summer. Borlaug needed to find somewhere else to grow wheat in the summer. Then he could run his experiments all year long. Growing wheat all year in different places would speed up the process. This was a new idea. Back then, scientists bred plants in one place.

STOP AND CHECK

What problem did Norman Borlaug work on in Mexico?

Some people call the Yaqui Valley the home of the "green revolution." This is because of Borlaug's work there.

Chapter 3
The Answer

Norman Borlaug was **energetic**. He traveled around Mexico. He was looking for a place to grow wheat in the summer.

In southern Mexico, he found two places that seemed perfect. They were the Toluca (*toh-LOO-kah*) Valley and Chapingo (*chah-PEEN-goh*). Now he could grow wheat all year long.

WHEAT-BREEDING SITES IN MEXICO

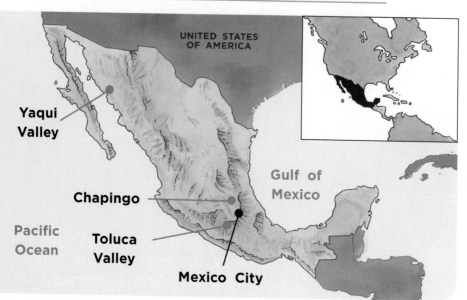

(t) Tinke Hamming/Ingram Publishing, (b) illustration: Peter Campbell

Local farmers helped Borlaug start crossbreeding different kinds of wheat in the Yaqui Valley. He observed the plants. He watched how fast they grew. He checked their resistance to disease. Then the best plants were crossed with other plants. This created new types of wheat.

In the summer, Borlaug moved these new plants to the farms in the south. Then he made more **observations**. And he crossbred more plants. Growing wheat all year long doubled the breeding rate of the wheat. Borlaug proved that his theory was correct!

Courtesy CIMMYT International Maize and Wheat Improvement Center

Borlaug (third from left) with a group of Mexican farmers in a wheat field.

Borlaug and his team developed wheat that **resisted,** or was not harmed by, rust. The **disappearance** of rust was exciting, but now there was a new problem. The grain on the new plants was too heavy for the stems. The plants often bent over.

The team started using shorter plants, called dwarfs. The dwarf plants had strong stems. The team crossed these dwarf plants with taller plants. They created a new type of wheat that had a strong stem. It also resisted disease.

AP Images

Norman Borlaug shows two kinds of wheat.

Norman Borlaug's work in Mexico was a huge success. He bred more than 40 types of wheat. These types of wheat resisted rust. They also had a high yield.

His system of breeding had another **benefit** too. The types of wheat he developed could be grown in many places around the world.

STOP AND CHECK

Why was Borlaug able to grow wheat all year long?

MEXICO'S WHEAT YIELDS

Wheat yield in 1945: about 250,000 tons

Wheat yield in 1965: about 2,500,000 tons

The wheat yield in Mexico increased after the new wheat was planted.

Illustration: Peter Campbell

11

Chapter 4
More Wheat for the World

In the 1960s, India and Pakistan could not grow enough food for their people. Scientists warned that millions of people could starve.

Borlaug shipped tons of the new wheat seeds to India and Pakistan. He also told the people the best way to grow the wheat.

MEXICO, INDIA, AND PAKISTAN

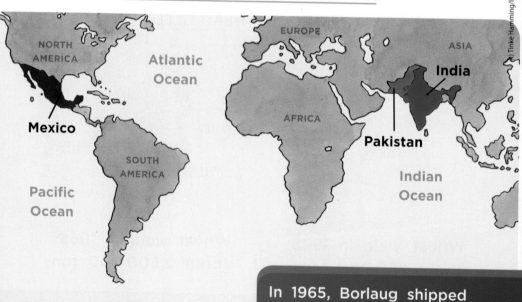

In 1965, Borlaug shipped 450 tons of the new wheat seeds from Mexico to India and Pakistan.

(t) Tinke Hamming/Ingram Publishing, (b) illustration: Peter Campbell

The new types of wheat grew well in India and Pakistan. More wheat grew. The grain yields **increased**.

Borlaug's seeds spread around the world. And his ideas began to **migrate**, too. In a **flurry** of activity, many plant-breeding stations were set up in other countries. Scientists shared their test results. They sent each other seeds. They changed their **behaviors**. They worked together as a community. This was something new.

The high-yield wheat grew quickly. But it needed lots of water and nutrients. Borlaug encouraged farmers to use **irrigation** and fertilizer. Together, the new plants and the new farming methods were called the "green revolution."

Borlaug taught scientists and farmers in India about the new wheat.

In 1970 Borlaug won the Nobel Peace Prize. Nobody had ever won it for growing plants before!

Norman Borlaug saved a billion lives. He showed people that science and technology could **transform** farming. Borlaug also helped to build a worldwide community of scientists. The scientists worked together to solve problems. The effects of Norman Borlaug's work are still seen today.

THE BLUE REVOLUTION

Before he died, at age 95, Norman Borlaug worried about a water shortage in the future. He called for a "blue revolution" to conserve water.

STOP AND CHECK

How did Borlaug's work help the world?

Borlaug's ideas helped people all over the world.

Summarize

Summarize the important events in *Norman Borlaug and the Green Revolution*. Use details from the text. Your graphic organizer may help you put the events in order.

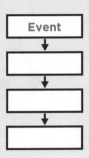

Text Evidence

1. In Chapter 1, what events led Borlaug to work as a plant scientist? Describe them in order. **SEQUENCE**

2. Turn to page 13. Find the word *community*. Use the information in the paragraph to figure out what the author means by *community*. **VOCABULARY**

3. Reread Chapter 4. Write about the sequence of events that helped increase wheat production in India and Pakistan. Make sure the events are in order. **WRITE ABOUT READING**

Compare Texts

Read a story about the importance of observing nature.

Golden  Apples

Each year, Lady Setenaya noticed a special apple growing on her apple tree. It took longer to grow than the others. It was also much bigger. Each fall the special apple shrank slowly.

Lady Setenaya watched and waited. Then she picked the apple while it was still ripe and juicy.

Over the years, she found many uses for the apple. When people bit the apple they became younger and kinder. A cream made from the core made people's skin softer. And people who drank a broth made from the apple's skin became happy.

News of the special apple spread. One day, a disease called Cholera visited Lady Setenaya. Cholera was disguised as an old man. He begged for a taste of the apple. Lady Setenaya saw through his tricks.

Lady Setenaya said no. She knew that Cholera would kill more people if he became younger. Cholera was so angry that he cut down the apple tree.

Lady Setenaya was upset. But she didn't really need the tree. She had studied nature. This had made her a natural healer. Lady Setenaya discovered new ways to keep her people healthy and happy.

Make Connections

How did Lady Setenaya investigate questions about nature? ESSENTIAL QUESTION

Why is knowing about seasons important in Norman Borlaug's biography and the myth *Golden Apples?* TEXT TO TEXT

Glossary

crossbreeding *(KRAWS-breed-ing)* breeding from two different types of plants or animals to produce a new type *(page 9)*

fungus *(FUN-guhs)* a type of living thing that survives by breaking down other plants and animals *(page 4)*

Great Depression *(GRAYT di-PRESH-uhn)* a worldwide economic downturn from 1929 to 1939 *(page 4)*

irrigation *(ir-uh-GAY-shuhn)* a system of supplying water to crops *(page 13)*

population *(pop-yuh-LAY-shuhn)* the number of people who live in a country, city, or region *(page 5)*

research *(ri-SURCH)* studying to better understand something *(page 6)*

yield *(yeeld)* the amount produced *(page 5)*

Index

Focus on Science

Purpose To find out about other plants that have been crossbred

Procedure

Step 1 With a partner, research plants that give us food. Many of these plants, such as corn and tomatoes, have been crossbred.

Step 2 Pick one crossbred plant to research. What traits did scientists want to create in the plant?

Step 3 Research the plant. Find out how it was changed. Where did it grow first? Where does it grow now?

Step 4 Use the information you found to make a visual presentation or poster. Share it with the class. Tell why you chose this plant.

Conclusion What have you learned about crossbreeding plants? How does crossbreeding plants help people?